계절의 향연
The Feast of the Season

계절의 향연
The Feast of the Season

구충회 제4시조집

Gu Chung-hoi's 4th Collection
of Sijo Poems

International PEN
Korean Center

시인의 말

사계절이 뚜렷한 지상낙원 한국
그래서 한국을 '금수강산'이라 부르지요
이곳에 천년의 역사가 숨 쉬고 있는
한국인의 전통시 시조가 있습니다
시조는 한국인의 얼이요 혼입니다
그래서 시조를 '민족의 꽃'이라고 부릅니다

시조에는 멋과 맛이 있답니다
고도의 절제미와 안정된 균형미
절도 있는 파격미와 태평스런 유장미
티 없는 담박미와 넘치는 해학미
K-pop도 트로트도 시조의 핏줄입니다

한국을 빛낼 아름다운 시조
천년의 메아리가 지구촌에 울려 퍼지길…

2024년 9월
대한민국 서울에서
구충회

|| Preface ||

Paradise on earth with four seasons, Korea.
We call Korea 'the land of beautiful scenery'.
Korea has the traditional poetry, Sijo,
with a thousand years of history.
Sijo is the spirit and soul of Koreans.
That's why it's called 'the flower of the nation'.

Sijo has its own style and taste
with great moderation, stable balance,
proper transition, carefree lifestyle,
pure simplicity, and sparkling wit.
K-pop and K-trot originated from sijo.

Oh the beautiful sijo that will make Korea shine.
May its echo of a millennium reach across the world!

September, 2024
Seoul, Korea
Gu Chung-hoi

|| Foreword ||

A Bounteous Feast Indeed

David McCann
(poet · translator · former professor of Harvard University)

An entrancing collection of sijo poems, Gu Chung-hoi's *The Feast of the Season*, is a feast indeed! Each poem, in his remarkable view of the natural and human worlds, will bring the reader into a place or a moment, and then, with that twist that all sijo poems are called to provide, give a new way to see and to think about it. Poet Gu shares a warmth and sense of humor at life's alterations, while also a sense of grief at time's passing.

The collection's first poem, 'The Way Spring Comes', starts the reader right off into the intermix of the human body and the realm of nature like this.

> There's a way in my body
> for spring to come in secret.
> At first sight, it wins me over,
> and then seeps into my vein.
> But sadly, it is visible
> only when I close my eyes.
>
> — from 'The Way Spring Comes'

Spring comes from outside the body, and at first sight – whatever that sight may be, as so many of the poems do explore and show – is welcome. But then it sinks down so deep within as to become invisible to the open eye. All that is there, sadly, becomes the memory, followed, then, by the glad sense of awareness with the eyes closed – of what it is that rests now deep within us – the poem!

And in a way that really drew my sense of connection, the poem 'Winter River' wraps these feelings and views together, as the poem turns from the abstract ideas of time, hatred, love and longing to a closer focus on the reeds by a river, there through the cold night, and then beyond them, the river itself, "crying deep inside".

Poet Gu shares a sense of helplessness in the face of the years passing, but through his poems, invites us to accept that reality, as he does. He remembers a childhood crush, in the poem 'Myeong-ja, My Flower,' and then how the cuckoo bird on Mount Paldal, in the peom Cuckoo Bird on Mt. Paldal, cries out for love, letting us all get a sense of the beauty and the poignancy of the natural world that surrounds us, and the human lives that fill it with their feelings and reflections.

And out there before us, the rest of the poems wait to win us over in Gu Chung-hoi's collection. It is a bounteous feast indeed.

September, 2024
David McCann

‖ 서문 ‖

참으로 풍성한 잔치

데이빗 맥캔
시인 · 번역가 · 前 하버드 대학교 교수

　매혹적인 시조집, 구충회 시인의 『계절의 향연』은 그야말로 축제 그 자체입니다. 각 작품들을 보면 자연과 인간 세계에 대한 놀라운 관점으로 어떤 장소나 어떤 순간으로 우리를 이끌고 갑니다. 그리고는 모든 시조가 그렇듯이 '반전'과 함께 우리를 새로운 방식으로 보고 생각하게끔 합니다. 구충회 시인은 시조를 통하여 변화하는 삶의 모습에 따뜻함과 유머 감각을 보이기도 하고, 속절없이 흘러가는 세월에 비애를 보이기도 합니다.
　본 시조집의 첫 번째 작품 「봄이 오는 길」은 인간의 몸과 자연의 영역을 혼합하면서 독자를 이끌기 시작합니다.

> 내 몸에는 남몰래 봄이 오는 길이 있다
> 첫눈을 사로잡고 핏줄로 스미다가
> 가슴을 적시는 그 길 눈 감으면 보이는 길
>
> 　　　　　　　　　－「봄이 오는 길」全文

　바깥에 봄이 오면 곧장 첫눈에 대환영이지요. 어떤 광경이 되건 많은 시詩들을 읽어 보면 그렇습니다. 그러나 그 후

눈에 띄지 않을 만큼 마음이 침울해지기도 합니다. 슬프게도, 그곳에 있는 모든 것이 추억이 되어 새록새록 생각나는데 눈을 감아보면 기쁜 마음이 들면서 마음속 깊이 내재된 느낌이 드는데 이게 바로 시詩가 되는 겁니다.

작품들 중에 정말로 제게 유대감을 느끼게 했던 작품이 「겨울 강」인데, 이 작품에는 그러한 감정들과 견해가 함께 서려있습니다. 시간, 증오, 사랑, 그리움이라는 추상적인 면에서 눈을 돌려 추운 밤 강가의 갈대숲을 주시하다가 그 너머 강으로 시선을 돌려 '(강물이) 속으로 울고 있다'라고 묘사합니다.

구충회 시인은 속절없이 흐르는 세월 앞에 무력감을 갖지만, 그러한 현실도 받아들이자고 우리 독자들을 다독입니다. 「명자꽃」이라는 작품에서는 어린 시절 그의 짝사랑이 나오고 「팔달산 뻐꾸기」라는 작품에는 팔달산 뻐꾸기가 사랑을 갈구하며 우는 모습을 떠올리게 합니다. 이런 작품들을 대하면 우리 주변의 자연에서 아름다움과 비애를 느끼게 되는데 우리네 삶은 그러한 자연을 보고 갖가지 감정과 회상을 갖는 것입니다.

그리고 제가 미처 평하지 않은 작품들도 우리의 마음을 사로잡으려고 기다리고 있습니다. 이 작품집은 그야말로 풍성한 잔치입니다.

2024년 9월
데이빗 맥캔

계절의 향연

The Feast of the Season

• 차례 •

시인의 말 preface 구충회 Gu Chung-hoi • 4
서문 foreword 데이빗 맥캔 David McCann • 6

제1부 봄이 오는 길
Part 1 The Way Spring Comes

봄이 오는 길	The Way Spring Comes	18
3월의 시	A Poem in March	19
선운사 동백꽃	Camellia Flowers of Seonun Temple	20
명자 꽃	Myeong-ja, My Flower	21
꽃바람	Spring Breeze in the Heart	22
황사黃砂	Yellow Dust	23
5월 아침	One Morning in May	24
카네이션	Carnation	25
실버들	Weeping Willow Tree	26
탁란托卵	Brood Parasitism	27
능소화	Trumpet Flowers	28
설중매雪中梅	Apricot Blossoms in the Snow	29
박꽃	Gourd Flowers	30
팔달산 뻐꾸기	Cuckoo Bird on Mt. Paldal	31
네잎 클로버	Four-leaf Clover	32
붉은 장미	Red Roses	33
수선화	Daffodil	34
연민憐愍	Compassion	35
새소리	The Chirping of Birds	36
낙화	Falling Flowers	37

제 2 부 여름밤
Part 2 Summer Night

여름밤 Summer Night	40
등대 Lighthouse	41
그린벨트 Green Belt	42
고향 생각 Thinking About My Hometown	43
바지락 Manila Clam	44
선풍기 Electric Fan	45
열대야熱帶夜 Tropical Night	46
폭우暴雨 Heavy Rain	47
잡초 Weeds	48
가뭄 Drought	49
꽃제비 국회의원 The North Korean Defector, an Assemblyman	50
하와이 연가 Hawaiian Sonata	51
자장가 Lullaby	52
위내시경 Gastroscopy	53
아내 My Wife	54
명품가방 식별법 How to Identify Luxury Bags	55
감자 Potato	56
한산도 Hansan Island	57
매미 소리 The Chirping of Cicadas	58
얼굴 Face	59

제3부 가을이 오면
Part 3 When Autumn Comes

가을이 오면 When Autumn Comes	62
아침 이슬 Morning Dews	63
만추의 연가 Late Autumn Sonata	64
억새의 춤 Silver Grasses Dancing	65
가을 Autumn	66
알밤 Chestnut	67
서릿발 Ice Needles	68
대추알 Jujube Fruit	69
가을 하늘 Autumn Sky	70
석류 Pomegranate	71
세레나데 Serenade	72
가을 산 Autumn Mountains	73
단풍 소묘素描 A Drawing of Autumn	74
모과 Quince	75
할머니의 하루 A Grandmother's Day	76
백자달항아리 A White Porcelain Moon Jar	77
청첩장 Wedding Invitation Card	78
나목裸木의 변辯 The Words of a Naked Tree	79
신혼 일기 My Newlywed Diary	80
지구를 보다 Looking at the Earth	81

제4부 눈
Part 4 The First Snow

첫눈 1	The First Snow 1	84
첫눈 2	The First Snow 2	85
첫눈 3	The First Snow 3	86
입동立冬	The Beginning of Winter	87
겨울밤	Winter Night	88
신도시 겨울 아침	Winter Morning in the New Town	89
황태	Yellow Dried Pollack	90
까치밥	Red-Ripe Persimmon Left for Magpies	91
눈길	Snowy Road	92
세한도 1	Winter Scene Drawing 1	93
세한도 2	Winter Scene Drawing 2	94
녹명鹿鳴	The Deer's Cry	95
겨울비	Winter Rain	96
겨울 강	Winter River	97
12월	December	98
섣달그믐밤	New Year's Eve	99
설	Lunar New Year's Day	100
노인병동 204호	Room 204 in the Elderly Care Ward	101
꽃게젓	Raw Crabs Marinated in Soy Sauce	102
담배꽁초	Cigarette Butt	103

제 5 부 황혼의 덫
Part 5 Twilight Trap

황혼의 덫 Twilight Trap	106
소망 Wish	107
인연 Perfect Match	108
촛불 Candlelight	109
약봉지 Pharmacy Prescription Bag	110
돌팔이의사 Quack Doctors	111
광화문 Gwanghwamun Gate	112
밤에 본 한반도 The Korean Peninsula Seen at Night	113
실버극장 Theater for the Aged	114
폼페이의 연인 A Couple from Pompeii	115
삼겹살 Pork Belly	116
메아리 Echo	117
요양원 일기 Nursing Home Diary	118
늙음에 대하여 About Aging	119
시조時調란 Sijo Is	120
상실喪失 Loss	121
인공눈물 Artificial Tears	122
만학晩學 Learning Late in Life	123
내 재산 My Assets	124
내로남불(아시타비 我是他非) Double Standards	125

작가 약력
번역자 약력

제1부

봄이 오는 길
The Way Spring Comes

봄이 오는 길

내 몸에는 남몰래 봄이 오는 길이 있다
첫눈을 사로잡고 핏줄로 스미다가
가슴을 적시는 그 길 눈 감으면 보이는 길

The Way Spring Comes

There's a way in my body
   for spring to come in secret.
At first sight, it wins me over,
   and then seeps into my vein.
But sadly, it is visible
   only when I close my eyes.

3월의 시

골목길 소문처럼 꽃샘바람 지나더니
만삭이 된 고양이 몸 풀고 조는 사이
병아리 하얀 햇살을 울밑으로 물고 온다

A Poem in March

Like a rumor in an alley,
  a cold wind blows in early spring.
After giving birth to kittens,
  a mom cat is dozing off.
Baby chicks bring the white sunlight
  in their beaks under the fence.

선운사 동백꽃

도솔천兜率川 단풍쯤은 환락가 웃음거리
구름 속 천년 세월 두 무릎 꿇어야만
하얀 눈 서방정토에 내려 주신 핏방울

Camellia Flowers of Seonun Temple

Nightlife hot spots may ridicule
   the autumn leaves of Dosol Stream.
A thousand years in the clouds, though;
   the red flowers are kneeling down.
The flowers fall like blood dripping
   on the white snow of Paradise.

명자 꽃

명자는 초등학교 5학년 2반 내 단짝
풋 가슴 동심 속에 아롱진 꽃 한 송이
황혼녘 노을 속에도 붉게 타는 첫사랑

Myeong-ja, My Flower

Myeong-ja was my best friend
 in class 2 of 5th grade.
In my childhood, I was so naive
 that I saw her as a flower.
My heart is aflame with love for her
 in the twilight of my life.

꽃바람

시집도 못 간다며 천대받던 우리 누나
꽃바람 살금살금 앙가슴 파고들면
연분홍 립스틱 바르고 어디론가 사라졌다

Spring Breeze in the Heart

My big sister was looked down on
 because she couldn't get married.
But one day, a spring breeze blew,
 making her heart flutter with joy.
Unnoticed, she vanished somewhere,
 after wearing light pink lipstick.

황사黃砂

일숫돈 찍으러 온 구두쇠 영감탱이
썩은 이빨 사이로 뱉어낸 누런 악취
봄마다 약속이나 한 듯 찾아오는 불청객

Yellow Dust

An old miser who comes to us
  every day to get money.
Yellow dust is like the old man,
  whose rotten teeth give off a stench.
When spring comes, the intruder comes,
  as if we made the appointment.

5월 아침

눈 시리게 영롱한 연둣빛 이슬이야
새소리 자지러진 봄의 소리 왈츠야
아니야 자연이 빚은 불멸의 환상곡이야

One Morning in May

The morning is like drops of dew
 sparkling brightly with a light green tint.
It's like a waltz in springtime
 with the birds chirping loudly.
Oh no, no. It's like a fantasy song,
 immortal, made by nature.

카네이션

골절이 시려오는 내 인생의 끝자락
선홍빛 카네이션 내 가슴에 달던 날
회한이 얼룩진 불효 꽃잎마다 맺혔소

Carnation

I feel painful in all my joints
   near the end of my life.
On Parents' Day, a carnation,
   brightly red, is on my chest.
Each petal causes me to regret
   that I wasn't good to my parents.

실버들

저것 봐, 휘감고 사분대는 저 몸짓
치맛자락 살랑살랑 바람결에 남실대면
아이구 남사스러워라 낯 뜨거워 못 보겠네

Weeping Willow Tree

Oh look at that, that gesture;
   the long branches sway to and fro.
They are moving like a skirt
   flying up in the breeze.
My goodness! How embarrassing!
   I'm too ashamed to lift my face.

탁란托卵

새 중에 뻐꾸기는 사기 치는 철면피다
뱁새 알 밀어 내고 제 것으로 바꿔놓고
뒤돌아 딴전 피우며 시침 떼고 뻐꾹뻐꾹!

Brood Parasitism

Cuckoo birds have a lot of nerve,
  playing tricks on other birds.
After pushing crow-tits' eggs
  out of the nests, they lay eggs there.
After that, playing innocent,
  they sing with joy, "Cuckoo, Cuckoo!".

능소화

불붙은 정념이 용암보다 뜨겁다
휘감는 욕망이 하늘로 솟구치면
나 그냥 숨을 멈추고 극락으로 갈 테다

Trumpet Flowers

Being burning with emotion,
  the flowers look hotter than lava.
If my desire soars high up
  into the sky like the flowers,
then I'll stop breathing and I'll die
  to return to paradise.

설중매雪中梅

바람결 매운 맛이 향긋하다 했더니
설중매 여린 가지 꽃망울이 터졌다
병아리 까만 눈동자 하얀 햇살 부신 날

Apricot Blossoms in the Snow

Oh the sweet scent from the blossoms
  in the wind, cold and bitter.
I see the buds burst open
  on the branches of the tree.
On the day, the sun shines so bright,
  dazzling the black-eyed chicks.

박꽃

순결한 척 청초한 척 호박씨 까더니만
하얀 달빛 쏟아 붓는 밤에만 피더니만
초가집 여기저기에 달덩이만 퍼질렀다

Gourd Flowers

Gourd flowers just pretended
  to be so pure and innocent.
But they bloomed only at night,
  glinting white in the moonlight,
Oh now gourds, resembling the moon,
  are here and there on the thatched roof.

팔달산 뻐꾸기

팔달산 뻐꾸기는 눈만 뜨면 울어 댄다
허기진 내 젊은 날 풋내 나는 사랑 찾듯
오늘도 초록에 헹군 이슬방울 토해낸다

Cuckoo Bird on Mt. Paldal

The bird cuckoos on Mt. Paldal
　as soon as it wakes up.
It still keeps craving for love,
　as I did in my young days.
Today too, it's seeking for love
　with dew drops on green leaves.

네잎 클로버

책갈피 깊숙한 곳 숨겨 보낸 마음은
순결로 맺은 언약 가슴 설렌 첫사랑
지금도 네잎 클로버는 몸 사르는 그리움

Four-leaf Clover

The book-marker deep in the book;
　my hidden heart was sent with it.
Oh the pledge made by purity;
　my first love made my heart flutter.
Even now, a four-leaf clover
　makes me feel a longing.

붉은 장미

사랑이 포로 되어 순결을 잃어버린
원부의 독침 끝에 응어리진 피눈물
애증의 세월을 건너 승화된 단심이다

Red Roses

A lady, obsessed by love,
   ever lost her purity.
So with poison in her heart,
   she held back her tears of blood.
Through the years of love and hatred,
   her heart turned into red roses.

수선화

육모 난 은 접시에 받쳐 든 황금 술잔
농염한 그 향기에 도취된 자기 사랑
요정도 뿌리쳤어라 물속에 핀 영혼이여

Daffodil

It resembles a golden cup
  on a saucer of six angles.
Attracted by its own scent,
  it's been in love with itself.
Oh poor soul, refusing fairies;
  it's in bloom in the water,

연민憐愍

생과부 허리춤이 아프도록 시린 날은
춘삼월 웃는 꽃도 볼수록 밉상이다
긴긴 밤 허기진 사랑 이슬 맺힌 여인아

Compassion

A grass widow has low back pain,
  suffering from her cold back.
So when flowers smile in spring,
  she starts to hate the spring flowers.
Oh lady hungering for love;
  tears mist the eyes for a long night.

새소리

수컷의 비명 같은 구애의 멜로디다
밤새껏 뜬눈으로 별무리 토해내는
핑크빛 세레나데가 윤사월을 울리네

The Chirping of Birds

The melody of courtship
  may be the scream from male birds.
With the eyes open all night,
  the birds invite a group of stars.
Oh, awesome! The serenades of love
  warmly welcome spring season.

낙화

정해진 이별이니 슬프다 하지 마라
순리의 미학이니 얄궂다 하지 마라
두 손을 모아야 하리 내 사랑 슬픈 영혼

Falling Flowers

The falling is a fixed farewell,
  so don't say, "I feel so sad".
It's the beauty of nature,
  so don't say, "It's ironic".
Now I'll put my hands together
  for the sad soul of my love.

제2부

여름밤
Summer Night

여름밤

개구리 소리 높여 제 짝 찾다 지친 밤
보채는 모깃소리 귓가에서 맴 돌면
쑥댓불 매콤한 내음 싫지 않아 정답네

Summer Night

When night falls, frogs start to croak
   so loudly to find their mates.
Mosquitoes are buzzing
   and hovering around my ears.
Acrid smoke from burning mugwort
   makes me feel good and I love it.

등대

미친 듯 요동치는 파도소리 사나운 밤
울부짖는 파도 저편 아스라한 촛불 하나
아들아 무사해다오 애가 타는 붉은 모정

Lighthouse

Wild waves roar, fluctuating
  so crazily during the night.
There's a candle flickering
  right beyond the howling waves.
"Oh my son, I hope you are safe."
  The mother is worried sick.

그린벨트

순결을 지키려는 초록빛 정조대다
개발이란 욕망이 호시탐탐 노리니
어쩌나 자손 대대로 물려줄 성역인데

Green Belt

It's like the belt for a woman
  to maintain her chastity.
The desire to develop
  is directed toward the land.
Good Heavens! For posterity,
  the holy land should be preserved.

고향 생각

별무리 총총하게 은하수로 뜨는 밤
모깃불 쑥 내음이 가슴을 파고들면
반딧불 꽁무니에도 파란별이 솟았다

Thinking About My Hometown

The Milky Way, a group of stars,
  was luminous in the night sky.
Burning mugwort, we made smoke
  to drive away mosquitoes.
Oh just then, fireflies emitted
  bright blue glows from their tails.

바지락

파도에 시달리다 진흙 속에 묻힌다
막힌 숨 신음으로 묵언수행 하다가
번뇌를 토악질하고 열반하는 사리다

Manila Clam

Suffering from the sea waves,
  it gets buried in the mud flat.
With a groan of suffocation,
  it meditates in silence.
And at last, spitting out anguish,
  it slowly dies, leaving gem stones.

선풍기

전기세 공포 속에 숨 막히는 열대야
가쁜 숨 몰아쉬며 목 빠지게 돌더니
몸통이 열을 받아서 분통만 토해낸다

Electric Fan

Tropical nights suffocating;
  electric bills will be too high.
Maintaining a breathless pace,
  the fan revolves so busily.
Its body getting awfully hot;
  it may explode in anger.

열대야熱帶夜

땀 냄새 찌든 하늘, 먼동 트는 새벽녘
선풍기 혼자 돌다 기진맥진 늦잠 들고
잠 설친 허연 낮달이 누런 하품 쏟아낸다

Tropical Night

The smell of sweat covers the sky
  till sunlight peeps in the east.
With the fan spinning around,
  so exhausted, I'm still in bed.
A pale moon yawns in broad daylight,
  as it spent a sleepless night.

폭우暴雨

염천이 녹아내려 폭염이 지친 자리
갈증이 말라붙어 사막이 된 황야에
빗방울 폭탄이 되어 폭포처럼 쏟았다

Heavy Rain

The hot weather seems over now;
   the heat wave isn't in full force.
The wild land is now a desert,
   where people feel a great thirst,
Just in time, heavy rain pours down,
   just like water cascading.

잡초

잡초는 본디부터 천출賤出은 아니다
밉게 보면 잡초요 곱게 보면 화초려니
왜 어찌 잡초뿐이랴 너도 나도 그런 걸

Weeds

Contrary to popular belief,
  weeds are not of humble birth.
If you hate them, they're unwanted;
  if you like them, they look lovely.
The thinking doesn't just apply to weeds,
  it also does to you and me.

가뭄

모심은 논바닥은 절망의 크레바스
흙살은 피 마르고 농심은 숯덩이다
아버지 흘린 땀방울 홍수 되어 넘쳐라

Drought

After planting rice seedlings,
   the rice field got hopelessly cracked.
Seeing the soil parched by drought,
   farmers became so frustrated.
Beads of sweat falling from my father;
   May the trickle become a flood!

꽃제비 국회의원

구걸로 허덕이던 시장바닥 꽃제비
목숨 걸고 탈북 하여 금배지를 달았다
서울 와 평양냉면을 처음 맛본 장애인

The North Korean Defector, an Assemblyman

The defector from North Korea
  lived begging at a market.
He'd risked his life to defect from it;
  now he became a lawmaker.
Here in Seoul, the handicapped man ate
  Pyeongyang cold noodles for the first time.

하와이 연가

은결로 감은 머리, 홍조 띤 볼우물은
야자수 초록 물로 새겨 넣은 내 문신
지워도 지울 수 없어라 그림 같은 그 얼굴

Hawaiian Sonata

Her wavy hair, silky and smooth;
  her dimples on the rosy cheeks.
They're like tattoos on my body,
  marked by water from green palm trees.
I can't get her image out of my head,
  as it's still vivid in my mind.

자장가

돌맞이 손자 놈의 쪽파 같은 발가락
새근새근 골다가 새소리에 꼬물꼬물
날마다 고 녀석 보며 자장가를 부른다

Lullaby

My cute grandson, one-year-old,
  has thin toes resembling chives.
Sleeping soundly, he sometimes snores;
  the sound of birds makes him wriggle.
Watching him, I sing lullabies to him
  every day with happiness.

위내시경

비수면 내시경은 눈 뜨고 우는 거다
무언가 꿈틀꿈틀 협곡을 파고들면
배 속이 뒤틀리면서 구역질만 토해낸다

Gastroscopy

Gastroscopy with eyes open;
  the procedure makes me cry.
Something strange snakes its way,
  like going down to a canyon.
When it does, I feel so nauseous
  that I think I may throw up.

아내

쓰레기 종량제로 가계부 구멍 난다고
임대주택 옥상으로 햇볕 한 줌 빌려다가
음식물 쓰레기 말리며 코를 막는 마누라

My Wife

The system, 'Pay As You Trash',
   makes her worry about our budget.
Our rented house has a sunny roof;
   she takes food waste to the roof.
While drying it there in the sun,
   she holds her nose due to the stench.

명품가방 식별법

비가 오는 날에도 눈이 오는 날에도
가방을 쓰고 가면 보나마나 짝퉁이고
가슴에 꼭 품고 뛰면 틀림없는 명품이다

How to Identify Luxury Bags

When it's raining or snowing,
  I can tell whose bag is fake.
If she puts it on her head,
  I am sure her bag is fake.
If she runs with the bag in her arms,
  I am sure it's authentic.

감자

삼복에 비바람이 응어리진 둥근 열매
쓰든 달든 평생을 숙명이라 여기면서
칠남매 가슴에 품다 불심이 된 울 엄마

Potato

Midsummer heat and rainstorms
　made potatoes firm and round.
Similarly, my mom lived out
　her destiny, sweet or bitter.
While raising her seven children,
　she seemed to reach nirvana.

한산도

제승당 깊은 밤은 달을 닮아 외롭다
충무공 홀로 앉아 나라 걱정 하시다
학익진鶴翼陣 펼친 그물로 왜병을 훑어낸다

Hansan Island

Deep in the night, the command post
 looks as lonely as the moon now.
Admiral Yi sat there alone,
 worrying about our country.
His tactic, 'crane wing formation',
 helped them defeat the Japanese.

매미 소리

태엽이 풀린 듯한 매미 소리 시들면
가을이 달려오는 숨 가쁜 메시지다
제 짝을 찾지 못한 채 하직하는 이별가

The Chirping of Cicadas

The chirping sound starts to die down,
   just like the clock being unwound.
It's a message, so urgent,
   that autumn comes in a hurry.
They now sing a goodbye song to us
   before they die without their mates.

얼굴

밤마다 달이 됐다 별이 되는 얼굴이다
내 가슴 비망록에 숨겨 놓은 사랑 하나
가슴이 시릴 적마다 꺼내보는 그 얼굴

Face

Every night the face in my heart
 is like the moon or like a star.
Oh hidden love, still remaining
 in my heart as a memory.
Whenever I feel melancholy,
 I recall the lovely face.

제3부

가을이 오면
When Autumn Comes

가을이 오면

한숨이 시름시름 곰팡이로 피어나는
달동네 우리 집 반 지하 월세 방도
아버지 깡 소주잔에 햇살 가득 담겠네

When Autumn Comes

Alas our room, half underground,
   smells moldy with our deep sighs.
To our room that's monthly rent
   in a slum, autumn will come.
Then my dad starts to drink alone;
   autumn sunshine will fill his glass.

아침 이슬

이슬이 풀잎마다 구슬처럼 맺혔다
세 살배기 손녀의 영롱한 눈동자다
또르르 구를 적마다 초롱초롱 샛별이다

Morning Dews

Every leaf in the morning
  is beaded with sparkling dews.
My granddaughter, now aged 3,
  has such eyes as bright dew drops.
Whenever dew drops roll off leaves,
  they're shiny like a new star.

만추의 연가

눈썹달 여린 달빛 연시가 머문 자리
억새풀 갈색 바람 외로움 파고들면
지워도 지울 수 없네 낮달 같은 그 사람

Late Autumn Sonata

The crescent moon casts a pale light
   on persimmons that are ripe red.
Silver grasses dance in the wind;
   loneliness pierces my heart.
Ah it's hard to forget the girl
   who resembles a daytime moon.

억새의 춤

늦가을 황혼녘에 억새가 춤을 춘다
백발의 춤사위가 윤슬보다 눈부시다
노년이 즐거워야지 춤추는 억새처럼

Silver Grasses Dancing

Silver grasses are dancing
  in the twilight of late autumn.
Swaying white hair looks more shiny
  than bright ripples on water.
Yes, that's it. Let's enjoy our old age,
  like the grasses dancing in groups.

가을

폭우로 씻은 하늘 쪽빛보다 푸르다
만삭이 된 벼이삭은 메뚜기와 노닐고
외다리 허수아비는 새 쫓기에 바쁘고

Autumn

The sky washed by the downpour;
   it looks fresh blue, not indigo.
When rice paddies turn to gold,
   the rice ears play with locusts.
The scarecrow, standing on one leg,
   is scaring birds away from crops.

알밤

봄여름 치성 드려 잉태한 여린 생명
철옹성 쌓아가며 애지중지 보살피다
섭리를 어기지 못해 떠나보낸 붉은 모정

Chestnut

Spring and summer passed with prayers;
   chestnut trees came into bearing.
Inside a fort of its own,
   each chestnut was well protected.
However, nothing breaks providence;
   the trees shed nuts with readiness.

서릿발

불에 달군 시우쇠 모루에 짓찧어서
밤새껏 날을 세운 시퍼런 칼날이다
하이얀 미소를 품은 원부의 은장도다

Ice Needles

It may be that hot irons
   were hammered on an anvil.
As if sharpened all night long,
   they're showing very sharp blades.
Oh heavens. I think of the silver knife
   that a girl holds with a grudge.

대추알

푸르락 누르락 누르락 붉으락
삶이란 그런 거다 변하는 게 인생이야
가시밭 헤쳐 나가다 쪼그라든 황혼이지

Jujube Fruit

First they're green, then they're yellow,
　and finally they're red when ripe.
Yes, that is what life is like;
　it is life that is changing.
While getting through all difficulties,
　they get wrinkled with old age.

가을 하늘

코발트빛 호수가 하늘에 떠 있다
흰 구름 한 두 송이 꿈처럼 피어나고
술 취한 고추잠자리는 정신 잃고 헤매고

Autumn Sky

There's a lake in the sky;
   its color is cobalt blue.
White clouds rise, in ones and twos,
   like the dream that also grows.
As if drunk, the red dragonflies
   are hovering aimlessly.

석류

봄여름 주고받은 밀어를 잉태했다
만삭을 짜개면서 비명을 지르더니
선홍빛 찬란한 생명 산통으로 쏟았다

Pomegranate

The fruit conceived the secrets
  spring and summer gave and received.
Then, at last, fully ripened,
  it split open with a scream.
The clusters of bright scarlet seeds;
  oh new lives came with the pain.

세레나데

언젠가 그 언젠가 풋내 나던 젊은 날
달빛이 스며드는 불빛 새는 창가에서
불현 듯 벙어리 되어 신음처럼 울었다

Serenade

Well, one day when I was young,
   wanting to do what I please,
I went up to her window;
   light streamed from it in the moonlight.
But, tongue-tied, I couldn't say a word,
   so I cried, as if moaning.

가을 산

몇 순배 돌렸기에 저리도 만취 했나
석양에 노을 섞어 폭탄주 마시더니
세월은 가는 거라며 인생도 가는 거라며

Autumn Mountains

The mountains seem to be drunk.
　I wonder how much they drank.
Wanting bomb shots, they may have mixed
　the setting sun with the red glow.
Oh they know time is going away,
　and that life is going away.

단풍 소묘素描

노을로 타는 잎이 선혈보다 더 붉다
스스로 때를 알아 제 몸을 불사르니
이승 끝 소신공양이 꽃보다 아름답다

A Drawing of Autumn

Autumn leaves in the sunset
   look much redder than fresh blood.
Knowing their time for themselves,
   the leaves set themselves on fire.
Late in life, bursting into flames,
   they're more awesome than flowers.

모과

생김새 투박하면 피부라도 고와야지
검버섯 흉하더니 네가 바로 나였구나
향수만 뿌리지 말고 마스크 좀 써보렴

Quince

If you are not good-looking,
   you'd at least have silky soft skin.
Your age spots look so terrible,
   but I think we look alike.
From now on, you'd better wear a mask
   besides giving off your strong scent.

할머니의 하루

생존의 무게만큼 폐지는 천근만근
골절로 뒤뚱대는 리어카 두 바퀴에
할머니 숨찬 하루가 노을 되어 감긴다

A Grandmother's Day

The waste paper she collected
　looks as heavy as her hard life.
With the weight of waste paper,
　her handcart is waddling.
　Out of breath, she finishes the day
　with the approach of sunset.

백자달항아리

보름날 솟아오른 덩그런 달덩이다
흥겨운 달 타령에 덩실덩실 춤을 추다
만삭된 우리 어머니 날 낳은 파안대소

A White Porcelain Moon Jar

It resembles the round moon
   that comes up on Full Moon Day.
When my mom was highly pregnant,
   she was dancing with full moon songs.
"Ah right then, I gave birth to you."
   So she said, laughing out loud.

청첩장

내 자식 결혼식을 나만큼 기뻐하랴
쓴 웃음 묻어나는 소집영장 아닐까
보내고 받는다지만 내 맘은 천근만근

Wedding Invitation Card

Who'll be happy just as I am
   at the news of my child's wedding?
Don't people think it's call-up papers
   that gives them a bitter smile?
Anyway, I'm uncomfortable
   with the practice of give and take.

나목裸木의 변辯

나목은 추워야 옷을 벗는 별종이다
겨우내 단련하여 몸맵시 날씬해야
꽃무늬 웨딩드레스 입어 볼 수 있단다

The Words of a Naked Tree

Taking off clothes only when it's cold,
  the naked tree must be a freak.
It insists it should be slim
  through training all winter long.
If it's so, a floral wedding dress
  fits its body as it wishes.

신혼 일기

돗자리 한 장 깔린 신혼집 월세 방
바위에 부서지는 파도소리 칠 때마다
"새색시 어디 아파요?" 노크하는 할머니

My Newlywed Diary

We, newlyweds, rented a room
   that had one mat, to live there.
Whenever hearing the waves
   shattering against the rocks,
with the words, "New bride, are you okay?"
   the old landlady knocked on our door.

지구를 보다

슈퍼문 큰 거울로 지구별을 살펴보니
온난화 덮친 자리 화상 입어 쓰리다
독감에 코로나 겹치니 달나라로 가야지

Looking at the Earth

The super moon, a big mirror,
   is looking at our Earth.
Global warming has triggered
   heat-related illnesses.
Severe flu and COVID-19;
   ah I will go to the moon.

제4부

첫눈
The First Snow

첫눈 1

첫눈은 은유로 찾아오는 느낌표다
선녀처럼 내려와 천사 같은 마음으로
단 한 번 순결을 주고 사라지는 마침표다

The First Snow 1

Indicating exclamations,
   the first snow comes as metaphors.
With the heart of an angel,
   white flakes of snow fall from heaven.
Only once, the snow shows purity
   and disappears, meaning the end.

첫눈 2

열일곱 가시내가 볼우물 짓던 날
내 입술 가장자리 첫눈이 내렸다
지금도 그 하얀 눈을 나 혼자 맞고 있다

The First Snow 2

When a girl, aged 17,
   smiled at me, her face dimpled.
Seeing her smile, I just felt
   the first snow fall on my lips.
Even now, thinking of the girl,
   I am alone in the white snow.

첫눈 3

첫눈이 올 적마다 반가워 맞다보니
어느 새 내 머리가 백발을 덮어 썼네
세월로 빛바랜 머리 핏기 가신 내 청춘

The First Snow 3

Every time the first snow fell,
  I walked around, welcoming it.
Ah, dear me, I soon became
  an old man with white hair.
As time passed, my hair lost its shine;
  alas my youth has stolen by.

입동立冬

목을 맨 메주덩이 누런 냄새 토하고
주름진 곳곳마다 곰팡이가 피는 방
홀아비 코고는 소리 문풍지가 떨고 있네

The Beginning of Winter

Soybean lumps are hanging inside;
  how disgusting the smell is!
Every crack on the lumps
  goes mouldy inside the room.
At the sound of a widower's snoring,
  draught excluders are shaking.

겨울밤

찹쌀~떡! 메밀~묵! 목소리 어는 소리
미아리 골목마다 메아리도 얼어붙은
옥탑 방 학창시절은 허기진 내 추억

Winter Night

"Sticky rice cake! Buckwheat jelly!"
   a vendor yelled in the cold.
In the alleys of Miari Town,
   even echoes seemed all frozen.
When living at the rooftop room,
   in my school days, I was hungry.

신도시 겨울 아침

토막 난 산허리 치맛자락 찢긴 자리
지역난방 아가리로 토해내는 구역질
시린 듯 파아란 하늘, 잿빛으로 시드네

Winter Morning in the New Town

The hillside, all dug away,
  resembles a torn skirt.
Because of district heating,
  foul smells come from the chimneys.
Ah alas, even the blue sky
  becomes pallid with the grey smoke.

황태

배 째서 죽이더니 내장까지 훑어낸다
혹한에 턱을 꾀어 하늘 보라 매달더니
눈雪으로 눈目을 가리고 공덕이나 쌓으란다

Yellow Dried Pollack

Their bellies were cut open;
  their intestines were removed.
With their jaws tied to the ropes,
  they are drying in cold winter.
When it snows, the snow covers their eyes;
  they're all ready for charity.

까치밥

가신 임 남겨 놓은 가지 끝 연시 하나
궂은 날 해로 뜨고 어둔 밤은 달이더라
그 임의 고운 숨결은 열린 하늘 높은 뜻

Red-Ripe Persimmon Left for Magpies

Red persimmon on the treetop;
  the deceased left it for magpies.
On bad days, it's like the sun;
  on dark nights, it's like the moon.
The warm heart of the deceased man;
  the open sky knows such meaning.

눈길

먹물 같은 어둠이 눈으로 환생 했나
산하는 신비스런 태곳적 정적이다
나 혼자 그 길을 간다 발자국이 외롭다

Snowy Road

Pitch darkness was born again
   as this white snow, I should think.
Mountains and streams are so quiet,
   like ancient times of mystery.
All alone, I walk on the snowy road.
   My footprints look lonely.

세한도 1

임이여, 하현달로 그려 놓은 박제였네
핏기는 노을 되고 뼈만 남은 저 기백
가지 끝 몸부림치는 승천이라 시리겠다

Winter Scene Drawing 1

Oh my dear, the waning moon
   seems to be stuffed in the drawing.
The flush of youth becomes sunset;
   just high spirits will be left.
Trying hard to ascend to heaven,
   the tree branches look lonely.

세한도 2

지천명 고개 넘다 바람 맞은 학 한 마리
송백松柏의 인연이라 세한歲寒도 푸르구나
이승 속 백팔번뇌가 응어리진 정토淨土다

Winter Scene Drawing 2

At the age of fifty
 a crane meets a mighty wind.
In harmony with pine trees,
 the winter scene is fresh green.
It must be the Buddhist Pure Land
 without 108 worldly desires.

녹명鹿鳴

먹이를 찾아내자 목청껏 우는 사슴
굶주린 동료에게 알려주는 메시지다
이렇게 아름다운 울음 세상에 또 있나

The Deer's Cry

When finding feed, the deer cries
   at the top of its voice.
The cry must be a message
   to invite its hungry friends.
Oh indeed, what a beautiful cry!
   Is there such cry in this world?

겨울비

지구가 변절 했다 눈 대신 비가 온다
정상이 비정상인가 비정상이 정상인가
지구가 열병을 앓고 있다 제정신이 아니다

Winter Rain

I am sure the earth has changed.
   It's raining, not snowing now.
Is it abnormal to be normal?
   Is it normal to be abnormal?
Ah the earth is suffering from fever.
   It must have lost its consciousness.

겨울 강

애증도 세월 가면 그리움이 되나 보다
여윈 나날 울다 지친 갈대숲도 시린 밤
강물은 소리도 없이 속으로만 울고 있다

Winter River

As time goes by, hatred from love
  seems to turn into longing.
Tired with crying for days and days,
  reeds look weak through the cold night.
The river, silently flowing,
  keeps its crying deep inside.

12월

오는 듯 가는 게 세월이라 했던가
미련도 후회도 앙금으로 남긴 채
또 한해 설원에 묻고 스러지는 낙조여

December

Is it said that time goes by
   as soon as it comes to us?
Leaving behind lingering feelings
   as well as lots of regrets,
one more year is being buried
   in the snow by the sunset.

섣달그믐밤

별빛마저 창백한 섣달그믐 시린 밤
등 굽은 그믐달은 모로 누워 자는데
쪽방 집 그 할머니는 무엇하고 있을까

New Year's Eve

On New Year's Eve, bitterly cold,
  even starlight grows pale and dim.
An old moon with a bent back
  is sleeping on its side.
The grandma who lived in the doss-house;
  ah I wonder what she's doing.

설

색동옷 입던 추억 나이테에 구겨 박고
무지개 부푼 꿈을 허랑하게 날렸어도
산하는 말이 없어라 황혼 빛이 서럽다

Lunar New Year's Day

Rainbow clothes I wore when young;
  growing older, I forgot it.
And I gave up a big dream
  of chasing a rainbow.
But silence from mountains and streams.
  I feel so sad at twilight.

노인병동 204호

숨소리 잦아드는 회색빛 심연深淵이다
가버린 추억들이 동공瞳孔을 맴돌다가
고사목 구름 스치듯 승천하는 쉼터다

Room 204 in the Elderly Care Ward

When inpatients breathe evenly,
  the room becomes a dark abyss.
Their memories, almost gone,
  start to hover around their eyes.
This shelter is where they go to heaven,
  as if dead trees touch the clouds.

꽃게젓

꽃게의 발가락을 아득아득 씹어댄다
엄니는 반평생을 잇몸으로 사셨는데
꽃게 발 씹히는 소리 가슴 아픈 메아리

Raw Crabs Marinated in Soy Sauce

I'm crunching crispy crab toes
   noisily, *crunch crunch yum yum*.
Having lost all of her teeth,
   my mom couldn't chew half of her life.
Ah the sound of chewing crab toes
   is echoing, making me sad.

담배꽁초

수시로 누런 냄새 빨아 먹는 청춘아
버리고 짓밟는 심사 모를 리 없건만
꿈 이길 시련 있더냐 몸 사르지 말게나

Cigarette Butt

Hey, young guys, how frequently
　you inhale cigarette smoke!
You throw the butts and step on them;
　I can guess what's in the mind.
However, don't be hard on yourself.
　Are there ordeals that surpass dreams?

제5부

황혼의 덫
Twilight Trap

황혼의 덫

불효가 쌓인 가슴 후회로 못을 친다
천륜을 허문 자리 회한으로 채우다
백발이 쌓인 머리에 황혼 빛이 서럽다

Twilight Trap

I wasn't good to my parents.
　Now with regret, I beat my chest.
Having broken the moral law,
　I am filled with remorse now.
My hair strands became gray with age;
　I feel so sad at twilight.

소망

백조 떠난 호숫가 무늬 진 여운처럼
햇살 고운 이른 아침 눈 시린 이슬처럼
해맑은 미소 지으며 하늘하늘 가고파

Wish

Like the ripples left in the lake
　where the white swan flew away,
like the dew shining in the sun
　so early in the morning,
now I wish I could go to heaven
　with a bright smile on my face.

인연

어릴 적 소꿉친구 학창시절 연인커플
부부로 다시 만나 한 침대를 썼지만
지금은 복지관 친구 신나는 댄스 커플

Perfect Match

She and I were childhood mates.
　In our school days, we were lovers.
We met again to get married;
　since then we've slept in the same bed.
Now we are the welfare center friends
　as well as dance partners.

촛불

스스로 고혈 짜내 몸 사르는 구도자
그 고통 눈물 되어 방울방울 맺히나
영혼이 승천하는 밤 홀로 피는 꽃이여

Candlelight

The candle burns itself slowly,
　as if it is a truth seeker.
The pain must be unbearable;
　the wax melts, dripping like tears.
On the night of the soul's ascension;
　oh the flower blooming alone!

약봉지

봉封마다 찍힌 숫자 저승 가는 번호표
밥 먹고 삼십분 후 허구한 날 먹고 나면
이승의 끝자락이라 하루 내내 아프다

Pharmacy Prescription Bag

The number stamped on each bag
   is the number to the next world.
Thirty minutes after each meal,
   I've taken prescription drugs.
Even so, I'm in pain all day;
   it's my last life in this world.

돌팔이의사

나이를 먹을수록 의사가 되나 보다
가끔은 전문의로 착각할 때도 있다
자신을 임상 실험한 대가大家들이 아닌가

Quack Doctors

The closer we're to old age,
   the more we're like doctors.
Sometimes we get the illusion
   that we are medical doctors.
We conduct clinical tests on ourselves,
   so aren't we all masters?

광화문

오백년 사직의 터 왕궁이 코앞인데
핏발 선 언어들이 비수로 꽂힐 때면
세종이 가슴을 치네 충무공이 탄식하네

Gwanghwamun Gate

Historic site of 500 years,
   the palace is right in the front.
The cruelty of people's words
   cuts each other like a sharp knife.
King Sejong is sad at their wrongs.
   Admiral Lee sighs loudly.

밤에 본 한반도

허리가 잘린 거야 심장도 멎은 거지
한쪽은 대낮인데 또 한쪽은 캄캄하다
어쩌나, 피가 돌지 않아 그 지경 그 꼴인 걸

The Korean Peninsula Seen at Night

The whole land looks split in half;
  I think its heart has stopped beating.
The South is as bright as day;
  the North is dark all night long.
Ah alas, it seems that's what happened
  because the blood didn't run well.

실버극장

꿈보다 추억이 아른아른 피는 곳
전설 속 사람들이 친척보다 그리워
나 혼자 그레이스 켈리의 푸른 눈과 마주쳤다

Theater for the Aged

It's the place to recall
   memories rather than dreams.
I miss the guys in the legend
   much more than my relatives.
All alone, I meet the blue eyes
   of Grace Kelly on the screen.

폼페이의 연인

화산이 폭발해도 껴안은 채 있더라
땅바닥이 빠개져도 떨어지지 않더라
이제 막 구름을 타고 솟구치고 있으니

A Couple from Pompeii

The volcano erupted,
  but the couple hugged each other.
The ground was cracked by the eruption,
  but the two didn't fall apart.
It was then that they were soaring up
  into the sky on a cloud.

삼겹살

겹겹이 쌓아 올린 세월이 안타깝다
세 치 혀 탐욕으로 목숨 잃은 불운이
불판에 다시 죽어야 살아나는 진미다

Pork Belly

I feel sorry for the years
   that have piled into layers.
Unluckily, pigs are slaughtered,
   as three-inch tongues are greedy;
They'll be born as a delicacy
   if they die once more on the grill,

메아리

에움길 굽이굽이 바람처럼 떠돌다가
황혼녘 길손처럼 골목길 맴돌다가
세월이 눈을 감으면 돌아오는 업보다

Echo

Roaming around like the wind
  in the windings of a crooked path,
hovering around the alley
  like travellers in the twilight,
the echo comes back as karma
  when it's time to close our eyes.

요양원 일기

가쁜 숨 몰아쉬며 초침은 달리는데
추사秋史의 서체書體 같은 아버지 저 육신
진혼곡 자장가 삼아 이승을 살고 있다

Nursing Home Diary

My father is scant of breath,
  but the clock is ticking fast.
His body looks like calligraphy
  that was written by Chusa*.
Requiem is a lullaby for him
  while he still lives in this world.

* pen name of Kim Jeong-hee (1786~1856), a master calligrapher of the Joseon Dynasty

늙음에 대하여

울면서 세상 만나 웃음 찾아 헤매다가
주름진 골짜기에 씨앗 몇 개 뿌려두고
해질녘 시든 하늘에 잠자리를 찾는 거다

About Aging

Crying loudly, I met the world,
  where I struggled to find laughter.
And meanwhile, I sowed some seeds
  in the valley, deeply furrowed.
Now I seek a place to sleep in the sky
  fading away at sunset.

시조時調란

마지막 손가락을 건반에서 떼어내도
잔물결 여울지는 노을빛 여운이다
내안에 여백의 미학을 확인하는 미소다

Sijo Is

After playing, I take my fingers
　off the keys of the piano.
But the music still lingers
　in my mind like a sunset.
However, sijo is like smiles finding
　the beauty of space in me.

상실喪失

내 몸이 나 같지 않은 날은 서럽다
부끄러운 남자의 고개 숙인 오줌발
어쩌다 꿈틀거리던 객기마저 시들고

Loss

I am so sad when I feel
  like my body is not mine.
Weak and slow urine stream!
  I'm ashamed of the weak flow.
Oh, sometimes, I'm full of vigor,
  but, in a flash, it weakens.

인공눈물

세상이 각박하니 인정조차 메말라
눈물을 아꼈더니 안구건조 웬 말인가
심안을 뜨고 나서야 업보란 걸 알았다

Artificial Tears

As the world is getting harsh,
  the people are hard-hearted.
I've saved my tears. What's wrong with this?
  I now suffer from dry eye syndrome.
Picturing it in my mind's eye,
  I realize it is karma.

만학晚學

새털같이 많은 날 바람으로 날리고
안개 낀 돋보기로 모국어를 새겨본다
요단강 여울목 밑에 각주를 달아가며

Learning Late in Life

As many days as bird feathers
  are all gone with the wind.
With the help of reading glasses,
  I bear in mind my mother tongue.
Not crossing the Jordan River,
  I add footnotes to what I read.

내 재산

결혼한 지 오십년 내 재산은 얼마냐
아들 둘 며느리 둘 손자 셋 손녀 하나
더 이상 바랄 게 있나 마누라도 있는데

My Assets

I've been married for fifty years.
   What on earth are my assets?
My two sons and their good wives,
   one granddaughter and three grandsons.
So for me, what more could I wish for?
   In addition, I have a wife.

내로남불(아시타비 我是他非)

나에게는 봄바람 남에게는 칼바람
눈동자가 기울어 사시가 되고 보니
이성은 허상이 되고 독선은 실상이다

Double Standards

As for me, it's a spring breeze;
  as for others, it's a sharp wind.
My eyes began getting droopy;
  seriously, I am cross-eyed.
Common sense is an illusion;
  self-righteousness is prevalent.

‖ 구충회 약력 ‖

시조시인, 수필가, 문학평론가, 문학박사
건국대학교 국어국문학과 졸업
고려대학교 교육대학원 국어교육과 졸업(교육학 석사)
가천대학교 대학원 한국어문학과 졸업(문학박사)

(現) 국가원로회의 원로위원
　　　세계전통시인협회 한국본부 부이사장
　　　한국시조협회 자문위원
　　　한국시조시인협회 회원
　　　한국문인협회 회원
　　　국제PEN한국본부 회원

시조집
『노을빛 수채화』『천년의 메아리』
『미네르바의 연가』『계절의 향연』
『여백의 미학』(동인지)

수상
세계전통시인협회 한국본부 작품상 · 학술상 · 시천문학상
한국시조시인협회 신인상, 한국시조협회 대은시조문학상
한국시조문학협회 작품상, 매헌문학상 대상

e-mail : kch-43@hanmail.net

‖ About the Poet Gu Chung-hoi ‖

Gu Chung-hoi (pen name: Dong-ho) is a sijo poet, essayist, literary critic, and a doctor of literature. He graduated from the department of Korean Language and Literature of Konkuk University. He obtained a Master of Education in Korean Language Education from Korea University. And then he received a doctorate in Korean Literature from Gachon University.

Gu Chung-hoi is now a senior member of the National Council of Elder Statesmen. And he serves as a vice president for the TPWAW Korea and as a member of the advisory committee for the Korean Sijo Association. Also, he is on the Korean Sijo Poets Association, the Korean Writers Association, and the International PEN-Korean Center.

Gu Chung-hoi has published five collections of his sijo poems: *A Watercolor Painting of the Sunset Glow*, *The Echo of a Thousand Years*, *The Love Song of Minerva*, *the Feast of the Season*, and *the Aesthetic of Blank Spaces*(coterie book).

Gu Chung-hoi received three awards from the TPWAW Korea: the Best Sijo Award, the Academic Award, and the Sicheon Literary Award. He also received the Best New Poet Award from the Korean Sijo Poets Association, the Dae-eun Sijo Poetry Award from the Korean Sijo Association, the Best Sijo Award from the Korean Sijo Literature Association, and the Mae-heon Literary Award(the Grand Prize).

‖ 번역자 소개 : 우형숙 ‖

현재 국제PEN 한국본부 번역위원장, 국제계관시인연합회 한국본부와 세계시문학회 번역위원으로 활동 중. 시조시인이고 영문학박사(시번역 전공)이며 모교인 숙명여자대학교 (25년)와 세종대학교(5년)(겸임교수)에서 영문학 및 번역을 강의.

시조시인으로서 개인 시조집 3권을 출간했으며, 번역가로서 한국의 시집 및 시조집 20여 권을 영어로 번역. 한국시조문학번역상과 국제PEN한국본부로부터 PEN번역상을 수상한 바 있음.

‖ About the Translator Woo Hyeong-sook ‖

Woo Hyeong-sook now serves as the head of the translation committee of International PEN - Korean Center. She is also on the translation committee of the United Poets Laureate International - Korean Center as well as the World Poetry Society. With a doctorate in English literature(major: poetry translation), she taught English literature and translation at her alma mater, Sookmyung Women's University for 25 years and Sejong University for 5 years as an adjunct professor.

As a sijo poet, she has published three collections of her sijo poems. As a translator, she has translated over 20 collections of Korean poems and sijo poems into English. She received the Korean Sijo Translation Award and the PEN Translation Award from International PEN-Korean Center.

e-mail: hyungswoo@hanmail.net

구충회 시조집

계절의 향연
The Feast of the Season

인쇄 | 2024년 9월 13일
발행 | 2024년 9월 20일

지은이 구충회
펴낸이 서정환
펴낸곳 신아출판사
주 소 전북 전주시 완산구 공북1길 16
전 화 (063) 275-4000, (063) 252-5633
E-mail sina321@daum.net
출판등록 제465-1984-000004호
인쇄·제본 신아출판사

저작권자 ⓒ 2024, 구충회
이 책의 저작권은 저자에게 있습니다. 서면에 의한 저자의 허락없이 내용의
일부를 인용하거나 발췌하는 것을 금합니다.

저자와 협의, 인지는 생략합니다.
잘못된 책은 바꿔 드립니다.

ISBN 979-11-94198-45-1   03810

$ 20.00

Printed in KOREA